Johnny, Don't Jump

A satirical comedy

Alan Ogden

Samuel French—London
New York-Toronto-Hollywood

FOR AMATEUR PRODUCTION ENQUIRIES

UNITED KINGDOM AND WORLD
EXCLUDING NORTH AMERICA
plays@samuelfrench.co.uk
020 7255 4302/01

Each title is subject to availability from Samuel French,
depending upon country of performance.

CHARACTERS

Johnny, a youth at the end of his tether
Tyrone, a middle-aged caretaker
PC Green, not destined to be chief constable; young
Judy Parker, a dedicated young journalist
Reverend Robinson, a little out of his depth; middle-age
Eileen, twenty, but untouched by Life
Raymond, a pushing youth, but lacking direction
Johnny's **Mum**, the cause of all the bother; forties

The action of the play takes place on a ledge around the top of a city office block

Time — the present

JOHNNY, DON'T JUMP

A ledge outside the top-floor windows of a city office block. Morning. Autumn

DC is the corner of the building, a narrow wall parallel to the front edge of the stage. From this wall, one side of the building stretches diagonally back towards UL and the other side goes back towards UR. Each of the two long walls has a large window in its centre. Upstage, the L wall meets a wall that runs at right-angles to it into the wings, as though the building were L-shaped. In front of the L wall is a ledge about three feet wide, which ends at the UL wall. The ledge has a parapet in front of it, about eighteen inches high, and wide enough to sit on. From DC the ledge continues round the R wall, but at that side it is much narrower, and has no protecting parapet

The ledge forms the acting area. It should be raised from the stage floor to give the illusion of being high up on a building. The area behind the windows is an office. It contains a desk with a telephone near the R window and one or two chairs. Access to the room is from stage L, behind the protruding wall. The characters gain the acting area by climbing through one of the windows

During the play, from time to time, a light wind blows across from L

When the play begins, Johnny, who is around twenty, unemployed and miserable, is sitting on the DS corner of the parapet with his back to the audience. He is writing on a pad of paper. He tears off a sheet, screws it up, tosses it over the edge of the parapet and begins again

Tyrone, the conscientious and phlegmatic caretaker of the block, appears in the office and sets to work to clean the inside of the window R. *After a moment or so he sees Johnny outside, and slowly registers amazement. He opens the window, and leans out*

Tyrone Hey! How did you get on that ledge?

Johnny Good-morning. Can you post this letter for me please? It's to my mother.

Tyrone What are you doing sitting on a window-ledge writing letters to your mother?

Johnny I'm getting ready to jump.

Tyrone You'll kill yourself.

Johnny That's the general idea.

Tyrone You don't want to go killing yourself.

Johnny Yes, I do. I've got nothing left to live for.

Tyrone You've got your mother.

Johnny You haven't had the pleasure of meeting her.

Tyrone If that's the way you feel, why are you writing to her?

Johnny You're supposed to leave a note, and there's nobody else to send it to. Will you post it for me? Then she'll get it first thing in the morning.

Tyrone Won't she get it quicker if you leave it here? She'll be called to identify the body.

Johnny Good thinking, but I've stuck the stamp on now.

Tyrone Does it matter? You won't need stamps where you're going. Your mum can steam it off and use it.

Johnny She doesn't use stamps, my mother. She doesn't write letters.

Tyrone Give it here, then.

Johnny It isn't quite finished. Hang on a minute.

Tyrone Have I got time to make a phone call?

Johnny If it's a quick one.

Tyrone Wait there 'til I get back.

Johnny Who are you phoning?

Tyrone Never you mind. It's none of your business. Don't go away.

Johnny Not 'til I've finished my letter.

Tyrone withdraws his head from the window, goes to the telephone in the office and dials 999. During the following, Tyrone is visible within, gesticulating as he talks into the phone, explaining the situation and being told to keep Johnny talking until help can be sent

Johnny finishes his letter, pulls an envelope from his pocket, puts the letter in it, tucks in the flap and addresses it. He looks around, rises and props the letter on the L end of the parapet, leaning on the adjacent wall. He looks over the edge of the parapet and moves DS

Tyrone (*into the phone*) Yes, sir. ... Yes, sir. ... I quite understand, sir. ... Yes. Thank you, sir. ... Right. (*He hangs up the phone, moves to the window L and looks out*)
Tyrone Er — pardon me. Is it all right if I come out and join you?
Johnny Feel free.

Tyrone climbs over the window sill and drops on to the ledge

Tyrone How do you do. I'm the caretaker of this block. My name's Tyrone. What's yours?
Johnny Oh yes. Telephoned the police, have we?
Tyrone (*innocently*) The police?
Johnny They've told you to keep me talking, haven't they?
Tyrone Well, if I'm to be honest, yes.
Johnny I wish people wouldn't interfere. I'm not doing anybody any harm.
Tyrone You will if you jump. That's the Directors' Car Park down there (*he indicates the DL area of the stage*) and it has to be kept presentable. They'll have me mopping you up, and I hate the smell of blood.
Johnny Is that all you care about?
Tyrone It isn't any of my business if you want to end it all, is it? Nothing personal of course. Now, if you're going, could you move round the corner, and go that way? (*He indicates the DR area*) That's only the yard where the dustbins are.
Johnny You're just like my mum, do you know that? Care about nobody but yourself.

Tyrone She's in for a shock, isn't she, your mum?

Johnny She doesn't shock easily. Besides, she wants to be rid of me. She isn't fond of me.

Tyrone But you've written to her.

Johnny (*darkly*) Yes. You read it.

Tyrone Me? I'm not reading it. I don't go reading other people's letters.

Johnny (*picking up his letter*) Well, I'll read it to you. I'd like your opinion. See whether you think it's all right.

Tyrone I don't know anything about suicide notes.

Johnny Neither do I. This is my first one. Listen. (*He reads*) "Top floor, Queen Victoria House, Bank Street. Dear Mum ... " Do you think "Dear Mum" is good enough? I wondered if it ought to be more sentimental: "Dearest Mother", something like that?

Tyrone Do you feel sentimental?

Johnny Not a bit.

Tyrone I should leave it as it is then.

Johnny Yes, I expect you're right. (*He reads*) "Dear Mum. I am writing to say goodbye. This might surprise you, but like you said I am nothing but a layabout and a drag so have decided to end it all. Sorry about calling you names last night but I was angry. I left my bedroom fairly tidy, but the sticky marks won't come off the lino near the window. Eileen can have my tapes and CDs if she wants them, or you might flog them if you need the ready. I left six pounds thirty-two under the clock by my bed with my kidney donor card. I don't expect my kidneys will be much use after I've jumped. I wouldn't be surprised if the council send you a bill for cleaning me off the pavement, as I expect there will be a bit of a mess. I won't be offended if you refuse to pay it. I hope you sort things out with Reg even though I still hate him. He'll be glad to get me out of his hair for good. Must close now. Hoping this finds you as it leaves me. Your affectionate son, Johnny". Do you think it's all right?

Tyrone Who's Eileen?

Johnny She's my girlfriend. Is it OK?

Tyrone It sounds all right to me. I would have thought you'd be writing a letter to your girlfriend.

Johnny We said goodbye when she threw me over. Girls always throw me over. (*He puts the letter back in its envelope*) In fact I've been rejected by the whole of society. I've got no family, no friends and no job.

Tyrone I don't have a lot of patience with pessimists myself. I'm not one for committing suicide every time things get a bit tricky.

Johnny It isn't a thing you make a habit of. (*He climbs on to the* L *end of the parapet*) Well, I'm off. (*He looks down*) Do you think you feel anything? You know, when you hit. In the split second before you splatter out.

Tyrone It's not something I care to think about. Come inside and I'll put the kettle on.

PC Green enters the office

PC Green (*calling*) Hallo, there. Anybody about?

Tyrone (*to Johnny*) They've arrived. Here they are. Hang on a minute. Stay where you are. (*He calls through the* L *window*) We're out here.

PC Green appears at the window

PC Green Ah ... er ... Good-morning.

Johnny Well, what do you want?

PC Green I've been sent to talk you down.

Johnny What do you think I am? A jumbo jet?

PC Green Do you mind if I come out there?

Johnny I suppose I can't stop you.

Johnny moves R *on to the narrower ledge*

PC Green climbs gingerly out of the L *window*

PC Green Windy, isn't it?

Johnny I hadn't noticed.

PC Green Is it all right if I sit down?

Johnny Please yourself.

PC Green sits on the parapet

PC Green Would you mind coming away from the edge? You
  don't want to go killing yourself.
Johnny Oh, but I do. It soon gets crowded up here, doesn't it?
Tyrone (*taking the hint*) I was just going in. I've got work to do.
Johnny Lucky you.

Tyrone climbs in through the L window

Tyrone (*as he goes*) Give us a shout if there's anything I can do.

Tyrone exits

There is the sound of a police car approaching and stopping

PC Green Keep everybody away from that room, that's all.
Johnny (*looking below*) Look. They've sent a patrol car.
PC Green They always send a patrol car to an incident like this.
Johnny Is that what I am? An incident?
PC Green That's right. They'll soon get things organized. Crowd
  and traffic control, that sort of thing. We don't want to snarl up the
  city centre any more than we can help, do we?
Johnny Don't we? I don't mind a bit of a snarl-up myself.
PC Green No, but then it doesn't affect you, does it?
Johnny It's me that's going to jump.
PC Green Yes. You're not being very considerate, are you?
Johnny I wasn't trying to be considerate. I'm at the end of my
  tether.
PC Green They all say that. We do our best to humour you, you
  know. Run messages and that. Would you like me to send for
  anybody?
Johnny I'll need an undertaker.
PC Green Oh, I don't know about that. You don't want to see an
  undertaker, do you?
Johnny I don't suppose an undertaker will be very keen to see me
  after ... You know — splat!

PC Green Very nasty. We do see some very nasty messes. You realize somebody will have to identify the body?

Johnny My mother.

PC Green She won't relish picking over the pieces for something she recognizes.

Johnny Nerves of steel, my mother. There's a letter for her there. (*He indicates the letter*).

PC Green That's thoughtful. A lot of them keep it in their pocket. Makes it difficult to read.

Johnny Do you do this often?

PC Green Oh no. You're my first.

Johnny Is that a fact? You'll be sort of feeling your way, then?

PC Green Yes, I am. Feeling my way. Playing it by the book.

Johnny Are you the best they could send?

PC Green The nearest. I was round the corner with my little bleeper. The fellows in the patrol car will be up in a minute.

Johnny Don't think I'm complaining. One policeman's as useless as another as far as I'm concerned.

PC Green Wouldn't you feel safer sitting down?

Johnny I'm not giving you the jitters, am I? (*He sits with his legs dangling outside the parapet*)

PC Green I wish you'd bring your legs over. You make me feel nervous.

Johnny swings one leg over the parapet and sits astride it

Johnny Is that better?

PC Green A bit.

Johnny If you're so nervous, what did you come up here for?

PC Green Call of duty, isn't it. Orders. "Young man up on a ledge threatening to throw himself off. Go and talk him out of it."

Johnny Why talk 'em out of it? Have you considered what you're doing?

PC Green I'm saving your life. It's in the Regulations.

Johnny But what for?

PC Green You're a young man with all your life before you.

Johnny That's what's getting me down. Imagine another fifty years of being unemployed.

PC Green Have you thought of joining the police force?

Johnny You're a right comedian, aren't you? They've got standards, you know.

PC Green They need healthy, quick-witted young men ——

Johnny Yes, I can see they're not getting them. But there's no way I want to be the tool of the idle rich, like you.

PC Green That's an ungrateful attitude to take when I'm trying to save your life.

Johnny You've no business interfering and saving my life. You don't care about me.

PC Green That isn't the point. It's my duty to follow Regulations. Would-be suicides should be dissuaded. And I earn myself a commendation by talking you out of it.

Johnny (*rising*) I'm sorry to disappoint you.

PC Green You're not leaving, are you?

Johnny There's nothing to stay here chatting for, is there? Will you see my mother gets this letter?

Johnny hands his letter to PC Green

PC Green Wouldn't you like us to bring your mother here?

Johnny I don't think that's a good idea. She doesn't like being disturbed when she's having a lie-in. (*He climbs on to the parapet*)

There is a murmur of voices from below. This continues thoughout the play

There's a crowd collecting down there, with your mates from the patrol car.

Judy Parker enters the office. She is a young, determined newshound with a vicious career ahead of her. She carries a camera

Tyrone pursues her on

There is a commotion

Tyrone My orders are *nobody* comes into this room!
Judy If the fuzz downstairs can't stop me, you're certainly not going to.

Judy looks out of the R window. She sees PC Green, but Johnny is out of her view

Judy Hallo? Oh, not the law. Have you driven him over the edge already?
PC Green No I haven't. He's round here. He's just going.
Judy Wait! (*She moves to the L window*) Come down off that ledge.
Johnny Who are you?
Judy Judy Parker, *Daily Trumpet*. What's your name?
Johnny Johnny. If it matters.
Judy I want an interview, and a picture. I'm coming out. (*She climbs out during the following*) I want you to answer a few questions. We pay well.
PC Green (*to Johnny*) It's getting crowded. Do you mind if I wait inside?
Johnny Please yourself.
PC Green Just shout if you want me.
Johnny Go plod your beat like a good copper.

PC Green climbs into the office. He and Tyrone go off L

Judy What's made you so desperate, Johnny?
Johnny Mind your own business.
Judy It is my business. Any good story is my business.
Johnny I'm not a good story.
Judy You will be when you've jumped. Come on, talk to me. Give us a break.
Johnny Nobody's given me a break.
Judy I've told you, we pay well. We'll pay anybody you name. Or your favourite charity.
Johnny What do you think this is? Sponsored suicide week?

Judy I've got twenty thousand readers out there who want to read your story.

Johnny No they don't. They've never even heard of me.

Judy They will. I'll see to that. It's great human interest. It's what sells papers.

Johnny (*an idea forming in his mind*) Let's get this straight. Are you telling me you're willing to pay me for answering a few questions?

Judy That's right.

Johnny How much?

Judy A lot.

Johnny More than a thousand?

Judy If I can have a picture too. Yes.

Johnny You can have a picture.

Judy You mean, you agree?

Johnny Yes, I agree. I'll answer your questions.

Judy Great. We'll talk while I take the picture.

Judy backs up to the UL corner of the ledge

Judy (*indicating DC*) Stand on the corner and face this way.

Johnny goes DC and faces L

Judy unslings her camera from round her neck and begins focussing on Johnny. She continues to focus and snap as they talk

Judy What brought matters to a head, Johnny?

Johnny You what?

Judy Right a bit, Johnny. What made you decide to jump today?

Johnny (*moving a little to his R*) I had another row with my mum.

Judy Further right.

Johnny If I go any further I'll fall over the edge.

Judy I'll try up here. (*She climbs on the parapet*) Better. Do you fight with your mum a lot?

Johnny She wants me out. She's got this boyfriend. I get in his hair.

Judy Can you get up on to that parapet?

Johnny climbs on to the parapet

Judy steps off on to the ledge, crouches down and aims her camera

Judy That's more like it. Don't you want to get out and be independent?
Johnny I can't afford it. I've got no job.

Johnny mimes and pulls faces as he tries to follow Judy's instructions during the following

Judy Right. Now, look at the camera. And I suppose living at home is cheap and easy. There's always a hot dinner on the table?
Johnny (*gazing at camera*) Hot dinner? Give over. Fish and chips if I fetch them. She doesn't cook.
Judy Oh? Now I want you to look distraught. Perhaps she's too busy cleaning and tidying after you?
Johnny Tarting herself up more likely. Trying to look like a teenager for that Reg.
Judy No, that's no good, you look barmy. Imagine you're wild with rage.
Johnny I am wild with rage.
Judy It isn't coming over. Too stiff looking. Can't you get yourself worked up? Think about all the things that make life impossible. Your mother, your girlfriend, your job. You're angry about them. You're in despair. You want to shout about it — to let the world know. Let it go, Johnny, let it go.
Johnny (*suddenly losing his temper*) This is stupid, you know that? Plain bloody stupid!
Judy (*clicking away with her camera*) Great! Terrific! Hold it! Marvellous! We got it.
Johnny (*stepping off the parapet*) I don't want to do this.
Judy Of course you do. That was terrific. Now let's get an action shot. Get up on the wall and face outwards.

Johnny climbs back on to the parapet and faces the audience

We hear a reaction from the crowd collecting below

Judy climbs on to the parapet UL *with her back to the adjoining wall*

Johnny Like this?
Judy Yes. Now make as if to jump. Bend and lean forward.

Johnny obeys

The crowd noise increases

> (*Aiming her camera*) Great. I've got the city street far below you in the background. Now turn your face this way and glare at the camera.

Johnny faces Judy and grimaces

> Hold it there.

Johnny wobbles on the ledge, in danger of losing his balance

Johnny (*wobbling*) Oh — oh — oh — oh — oh — ooops! (*He recovers his balance and drops back on to the ledge*) Wow! That was a near thing.
Judy Pity. I'd have got the most terrific action shot if you hadn't pulled back.
Judy Sorry, I'm sure.
Judy Try again.
Johnny One more time. I'm getting bored. (*He poses again*)

Judy aims her camera

> *Rev. Robinson enters the office within and crosses to the* R *window*

Judy Right. Hold it. Face this way. Glare harder.

Rev. Robinson puts his head out of the R *window. Judy and Rev. Robinson are hidden from each other by the corner of the building*

Rev. Robinson Wait, my boy, wait. Life is too precious to be thrown away.

Judy Oh God. Who's that?

Johnny (*relaxing his pose*) Some fool of a vicar.

Rev. Robinson (*putting one leg over the window sill*) Do let me talk to you first. Things are never as bad as they seem.

Johnny They're getting worse by the minute. Stay where you are or I'll jump.

Rev. Robinson Oh, my! I won't move another inch. (*He freezes*)

Johnny (*to Judy*) Did you get your picture?

Judy No.

Johnny (*to Judy*) Third time lucky then. Come on. (*He poses again*)

Judy puts the camera to her eye

Rev. Robinson (*putting his other leg over the sill*) I say! Don't do it! Don't do it! It isn't right.

Johnny (*over his shoulder*) Stay where you are.

Rev. Robinson scrambles from the window and hitches along the ledge

Rev. Robinson (*as he moves*) No! No! No!

Judy snaps the camera

Judy Got it.

Rev. Robinson reaches the corner, leaps forward and grabs Johnny. They almost go over the edge together. Judy grabs them both

Johnny (*yelling*) Lay off! Lay off!

They all separate

Judy (*to Rev. Robinson*) What did you want to do that for?

Rev. Robinson He almost killed himself.
Johnny I was posing for a photograph. (*To Judy*) Did you get it?
Judy Yes. It should be a beaut. See you.

Judy makes for the L window

Johnny Hey! We haven't finished the interview.
Judy I've got all I need.
Johnny What about my money?
Judy Oh yes. Who do I send it to?
Johnny I'll have it myself please.
Judy I can't send money where you're going.
Johnny I'm not going now. I can start up in business with a
  thousand pounds. Start a new life.
Judy You can't do that.
Rev. Robinson Excuse me, but am I on the right ledge? You are the
  potential suicide, aren't you?
Johnny Not any longer. She's going to pay me a thousand pounds
  for my story.
Judy No I'm not. Not if you don't jump.
Johnny But you said you've got twenty thousand readers waiting
  to read it.
Judy Look. "Despair Drives Youth to Suicide" makes news. It sells
  papers. Especially with pictures. But "Suicidal Youth changes
  His Mind" isn't a story at all.
Johnny It's human interest.
Judy Human — yes. Interest — no. Human interest is death and
  disaster. Accidents and suicides. Robbery and murder. It isn't the
  good news that boosts circulation.
Johnny So I don't get my money?
Judy Sorry, feller, that's the way it is. Life's hard. You want the
  money, you've got to be the one to jump.
Rev. Robinson I hope I misunderstand you. You seem to be
  inciting this young man to kill himself. That is a criminal offence.
Judy Go say your prayers. (*She climbs into the office through the
  L window during the following*)

Johnny (*bitterly*) While you're at it, you might as well go over the road and get behind one of those windows. You'll get a picture of me on the way down.

Judy No, the TV boys do that better. They're setting up right now. They'll have a camera follow you as you fall. Action shot. Then they can play it back in slow motion. Great stuff.

Judy goes in and exits L

Johnny She's conned me. I thought she saw me as a human being.

Rev. Robinson Do you think we could move over a bit? The altitude's making me dizzy.

Johnny You'd better sit down.

Rev. Robinson That might be a good idea.

Rev. Robinson sits on the parapet, glances over the edge and is terrified. He rises and leans his back against the wall

Rev. Robinson On second thoughts ——

Johnny You do look a bit pale.

Rev. Robinson Could we go inside, do you think?

Johnny There's nothing to stop you going in. When I leave here I'm going that way. (*He points over the edge*)

Rev. Robinson Oh no, my dear friend. Do think again. Think what you're throwing away.

Johnny sits astride the parapet, L

Johnny What am I throwing away?

Rev. Robinson Life itself. That most precious of gifts.

Johnny Thousands of people die every day. What's one more?

Rev. Robinson But it is not up to us to choose *when* to die. Life may be a battle, but you don't surrender a battle at the first setback.

Johnny Oh yes? "Onward Christian Soldiers" and all that?

Rev. Robinson Exactly. "Fight The Good Fight". Life's little battles strengthen the character.

Johnny I've been battling with my mum for twenty years, and that doesn't seem to have strengthened my character. Look at me. I'm twenty, I'm idle and I'm useless.

Rev. Robinson Nobody is useless. Nobody.

Johnny You ask my mum about that. She'll tell you. Ask my teachers when I was at school. You should have seen them smile when I failed all my exams. Gave them a chance to say "I told you so." Ask all the bosses I've worked for. They all got rid of me, didn't they?

Rev. Robinson So what is your trade?

Johnny Trade? Vicar, what planet do you live on? I've done labouring and I've done packing. And once I was on the dustcarts for a bit. But I haven't got a trade. I can't do anything. Except ——

Rev. Robinson Yes? Except?

Johnny Well, I was a delivery man for a week. I can drive. Passed my test first time. Reg taught me. Only good thing he ever did. He was making a good impression on my mum.

Rev. Robinson Who is Reg?

Johnny My mum's boyfriend.

Rev. Robinson Ah. You get on well with Reg, do you?

Johnny He hates the sight of me. So does my mum. They want me out. I think I remind them of my dad.

Rev. Robinson What happened to your dad?

Johnny Don't know. He walked out. I don't think she was married to him.

Rev. Robinson Don't you know?

Johnny How would I? You don't go asking your mother for her wedding certificate, do you? (*He swings his leg over the parapet so that he is facing outwards*)

Rev. Robinson Oh please. I wish you'd come away from that edge.

Johnny Worries you, does it? (*He swings round, brings up his right leg with his knee bent and his foot on the parapet, then lies back with his left leg still dangling*) Heights don't bother me. (*He draws up his left leg and turns over on to his face*)

Rev. Robinson (*leaping forward*) No! No! (*He realizes how near to the edge he is and moves back again*) Please don't do that.

Johnny (*looking up over his shoulder*) You've gone green. You're
   not cut out for this, are you? (*He sits up*) Well, what do you
   suggest, then? Where do I go from here? Any ideas?
Rev. Robinson You sound to have had a variety of experiences —
   but I honestly think the Job Centre might be more use that I can
   be.
Johnny You undervalue yourself, vicar. Nobody could be as
   useless as that.

Eileen enters the office from L *carrying a brown paper bag.*
Tyrone follows her on

Eileen crosses to the R *window*

Eileen (*calling*) Johnny? Johnny, are you there?
Johnny (*rising*) Eileen?

Tyrone comes to the L *window*

Tyrone I can't keep 'em away. You don't know how popular you
   are. This one says she's your girlfriend.
Eileen Johnny, it's me.
Johnny Eileen, what are you doing here?
Eileen I've come to say goodbye.
Johnny Why? Where are you going?
Eileen Don't be daft, Johnny. *I'm* not going anywhere.
Johnny But you said you never wanted to see me again.
Eileen That was before.
Johnny Before?
Eileen Can I come out there?
Johnny If you like.
Eileen It looks ever so narrow.
Johnny It's wider round this side.
Eileen Hang on then.

Inside the room, Eileen moves to the L *window*

Eileen Give us a hand, Johnny.
Tyrone I'll give you a helping hand, miss.
Eileen You keep your hands to yourself.

Eileen climbs out of the window, helped by Johnny. Eileen shows a great deal of leg. Tyrone and Rev. Robinson observe her closely

Tyrone (*winking at Johnny*) Lucky lad. (*To Rev. Robinson*) Hallo, your reverence. You haven't got blown away, then?
Eileen It is windy, isn't it?
Johnny You didn't have to come.
Eileen I'm not complaining. It's nice. (*She sits on the parapet*) You could sunbathe.

Eileen leans back against the L wall and puts one leg up on the parapet

Rev. Robinson Well — er — you seem to have found a young person who understands you much better than I do. Your own generation.
Johnny That's all right, vicar. You go and open your jumble sale, or whatever. I wouldn't want to keep you from your duties.
Rev. Robinson You do understand ——
Johnny Better than you think. Goodbye, vicar.
Rev. Robinson Goodbye then, and — er — (*he starts to say "God bless you" but changes his mind*) — G — Good luck.

Rev. Robinson is helped through the window by Tyrone and they both exit L

Eileen What a funny little man.
Johnny He doesn't like heights. Won't like Heaven, will he?

Eileen laughs

Be careful you don't fall.
Eileen (*looking over the edge*) It's a long way down, isn't it? You could kill yourself.

Johnny Yes.

Eileen (*remembering*) Oh yes. What a thing to say! (*She giggles*) I'm not very tactful, am I? Oh look, I brought you some grapes. They're seedless. (*She holds the paper bag out to Johnny*)

Johnny What did you want to go bringing grapes for? You're insensitive, do you know that?

Eileen I wanted to show my sympathy. And I thought a bunch of flowers was a bit too much like a funeral under the circumstances.

Johnny You didn't have to bring flowers or anything. I don't want anything, do I? What a waste.

Eileen You don't really want to jump, Johnny.

Johnny You're the third person who's said that. Everybody's very clever, aren't they? Everybody knows what I want better than I know myself.

Eileen What good will it do, killing yourself?

Johnny A lot of good. I won't have anything to worry about any more.

Eileen You never said you worry about things.

Johnny Well, of course I worry about things. Why do you think I've got into this state? You don't go jumping off roofs if you aren't worrying about things, do you?

Eileen You're mentally unbalanced, Johnny. You're sick. You've gone round the twist. They should put you in hospital.

Johnny I don't need to go into hospital. It's the mortuary I'm going to.

Eileen Chapel of rest.

Johnny Mortuary. In a refrigerator.

Eileen I'm not visiting a refrigerator. If they lay you out in a chapel of rest I'll come and visit you. I can wear that black dress that you like that I got in the sales.

Johnny You can't wear that in a chapel of rest. It's got no back in it.

Eileen I've never talked to anybody who's mental before.

Johnny Stop saying I'm mental.

Eileen It's what the inquest will say. "Suicide while the balance of his mind was disturbed".

Johnny You don't know what you're talking about.

Eileen Oh, yes, I do. It's so your mum will get your insurance money.

Johnny I haven't got any insurance.

Eileen Oh, Johnny! Who's going to pay for your funeral?

Johnny I don't know. The newspapers can pay. I've sold my story to the *Daily Trumpet*.

Eileen What story?

Johnny I don't know what story. They'll make it all up. But she took my photograph.

Eileen Are you going to have your picture in the paper?

Johnny Yes. And on TV.

Eileen (*enviously*) Oh, Johnny!

Johnny (*pointing*) They're setting up over there somewhere.

Eileen Oh, I can see them, down in that window. Look, there's the camera. (*She waves*) Do you think they'll put my picture in the paper too? "Suicide's grieving girlfriend", that kind of thing?

Johnny I'm going to kill myself, you know. I'm going to leap from this ledge and bash my brains to pulp on the pavement, and all you're concerned about is getting your picture in the paper. You don't care.

Eileen I do care. You're going to kill yourself because of me. I'll never forget that. It's so romantic.

Johnny It isn't because of you at all. It's because I hate myself. And it isn't romantic, it's tragic.

Eileen I'll be famous for days. Everybody will be ever so sorry for me.

Johnny It's me they should be sorry for.

Eileen (*looking over the parapet*) Look, Johnny, they've cordoned off the car park down there. Isn't that thoughtful? They don't want anybody to get hurt when you jump.

Johnny (*looking over*) I hate people.

Eileen You don't. Wave to them, Johnny.

Johnny waves. The background hum of voices gets louder

Eileen There. Some of them are waving back.

Johnny I'll give them something to wave for.

Johnny climbs on to the parapet at the UL end. The voices die away to silence. Johnny "tightrope walks" along the parapet to DC

Faintly an official voice over a loud-hailer can be heard

Voice (*off*) Stand back, please. Stand back, madam. This is not a circus.

Johnny turns at the DC end, but begins to lose his balance. He rocks and waves his arms. The crowd gasps; there is a distant scream, then utter silence

Johnny Oh! Oh! A — A — A — A — Ah! (*He drops safely back on to the ledge*)

The voices re-start loudly, then die to a hum

Johnny Whoops. That was a near thing. Gave me quite a turn.
Eileen It gave me a turn too. I don't want you to die, Johnny.
Johnny Don't you? Do you mean there's a chance we could get together again?

Raymond, an earnest-looking youth about Johnny's age, enters the office and crosses to the R window

Eileen There might be a chance if ——
Johnny If there was a chance, I might decide not to jump.
Raymond (*at the window*) Excuse me! Excuse me!
Johnny What is it?
Raymond You must be Johnny.
Johnny Must I?
Raymond I'm Raymond. Mind if I join you?
Johnny It's a free country.

Raymond climbs out on to the ledge, seeming not to notice the danger. He edges towards Johnny and holds out his hand

Raymond Nice to meet you. Windy, isn't it? (*To Eileen*) Hallo.
Eileen Hallo.
Raymond (*after a second look*) Hall-o!
Johnny This is Eileen. She's my girlfriend.

Eileen Was.

Johnny I thought ——

Raymond You're a lucky girl. He's a brave man, your Johnny. He's got principles.

Eileen Has he?

Johnny Are you another reporter?

Raymond Oh no. I'm in the same boat as you are. I do admire what you're doing. It's time somebody made them take notice.

Johnny Made who?

Raymond Them. Society.

Johnny I don't understand you.

Raymond They're all talking about you down there. You're making a protest, aren't you?

Johnny Am I?

Raymond You symbolize a betrayed generation.

Johnny Who, me?

Raymond You're sacrificing yourself so that others may be saved from having to suffer as you have suffered.

Johnny Thanks for telling me.

Eileen Is that what they're saying down there?

Raymond More or less. I'm interpreting it in a manner of speaking. But that's the general idea.

Johnny I don't think you quite understand. I'm at the end of my tether.

Raymond That's right.

Eileen The balance of his mind's gone.

Raymond Precisely. Well it would.

Johnny I feel rejected. Nobody loves me.

Raymond I know precisely how you feel.

Johnny Who the bloody hell are you?

Raymond I'm a fellow sufferer. Another normal, average unemployed human being with normal, average human feelings and abilities. Another reject. Another victim of the de-humanized, consumer-conscious, profit-motivated, computer-orientated bureaucracy that we live in.

Eileen Oh, you've got a lovely way of expressing yourself.

Raymond And you've got very pretty hair, if I may say so.

Eileen (*simpering*) You may say so. I've gone on to a new shampoo. Do you like the smell? I think it's lovely.

Johnny Shut up about shampoo. (*To Raymond*) Are you trying to sell me insurance or something?

Raymond (*embracing Johnny*) I've come to join you, brother!

Johnny Get off me. What's the matter with you?

Raymond It's going to be a double suicide. It'll be sensational.

Johnny I'm not making a suicide pact with a complete stranger.

Raymond We're not strangers. We share the same ideals. That makes us brothers in adversity.

Eileen (*impressed*) There, Johnny.

Johnny I haven't got any ideals. I just want to be wanted.

Raymond We all want to be wanted, that's our tragedy. By dying here today we will symbolize the despair at the heart of the youth of all the western nations. The sickness at the centre of society; the canker at the core, the ——

Johnny The misery in the middle?

Raymond Don't laugh. Suicide is the supreme sacrifice.

Johnny I'm not laughing. I thought of it first — remember?

Eileen He's only trying to be helpful, Johnny.

Johnny It would be helpful if he went away. I prefer to be miserable on my own

Raymond You're being a bit self-centred, aren't you?

Eileen He's always been self-centred. I told him but he doesn't listen. He's always been one to go his own way regardless.

Raymond (*to Johnny*) That isn't the way to gain sympathy, you know.

Eileen That's exactly what I tell him.

Raymond It only alienates people.

Eileen (*who hasn't met "alienates" before*) Yes, I'm sure it does, Johnny.

Johnny All right. All right. If you want it to be a party, why don't we all go together? (*He climbs on to the parapet*)

There are gasps from the crowd below

Eileen Oh Johnny! No!

Raymond A triple suicide? That really would be something. (*To Eileen*) What do you say?

Eileen I don't know. I do admire you, don't think I don't.

Raymond Do you?

Eileen Oh yes. You're so masterful. But I wasn't thinking of committing suicide at this moment in time.

Raymond You mean you aren't in the depths of despair?

Eileen I can't say I am. I quite enjoy life, really.

Raymond Enjoy it? Despite everything?

Eileen What everything?

Raymond You know — everything. Unemployment, wars, famine, pollution, the greenhouse effect, the government ——

Eileen Oh that. I don't think about all that.

Raymond Not ever?

Eileen Not ever.

Raymond You know, you really are an inspiration.

Eileen Oh, do you think so?

Raymond You're so calm, so tranquil, so self-possessed, so ——

Johnny So thick?

Eileen Johnny, why don't you jump and have done with it?

Raymond I'd love to know how you arrived at your philosophy of life.

Eileen I don't know if I could explain, really.

Raymond Would you like to try? Over a cup of coffee?

Eileen Oh yes. I think I would.

Raymond How about the McDonald's round the corner?

Eileen Lovely.

Raymond Now?

Eileen Why not?

Raymond (*making for the window,* L) Come on then.

Johnny Here! What about our Great Gesture To The World?

Raymond Another time, feller. (*To Eileen*) Can you make it?

Eileen (*climbing through the window*) Thank you. It's nice to be escorted by a gentleman. Bye, Johnny. Have a nice day.

Raymond (*climbing after Eileen*) Bye, old lad. I shall always be grateful to you for bringing us together.

Eileen and Raymond cross the office and exit

Johnny (*calling after them*) And may all your troubles be little
mutations! (*He remains standing on the parapet. He contemplates
leaping, then he climbs down*)

There are suitably disappointed noises from the crowd

Johnny tries walking along the narrow ledge to the R *window*

*Mum, Johnny's mother, enters the office with Tyrone at her
elbow. With Johnny out of her view she comes to the* L *window and
looks out*

Mum Johnny? Oh my God, he's done it.
Tyrone Don't panic, he'll be round the corner. Other window.

Mum moves to the R *window as Johnny, having heard her voice,
returns to the wide ledge*

Mum (*at the* R *window*) He's not here.
Johnny (*moving* DC) Is that you, Mum?
Mum Oh, you frightened me, Johnny. I thought you'd gone.
Johnny Any minute now, Mum.
Mum You don't mean it, Johnny.
Johnny I wish people would stop telling me I don't mean it. I mean
it.
Mum They brought me your letter. Look. (*She holds out Johnny's
letter, out of its envelope*) You shouldn't write letters like that to
your mother. Why do you want to be so stupid, Johnny?
Johnny I can't help being stupid. You said so. I'm a great stupid
lump and I take after my father.
Mum I didn't mean it. Come back inside.
Johnny No. If you want to talk to me, you come out here.

Johnny moves L, *out of his mother's view*

Mum Out there? I'm not coming out there. It's dangerous.
Johnny OK then. I'm going.

Mum moves to the L window

Mum Johnny! How can you treat your own mother like this?

Johnny moves to the dead end UL and climbs on to the parapet

We hear the crowd react

Johnny That's all you care about, isn't it? How it affects you. Bye,
Mum.

*With his back against the end wall Johnny raises his left leg in the
air as though about to step into space*

The crowd gasps

Mum Johnny! I'm coming out! I'm coming out. (*She sits on the
window sill, her legs outside the building*) Help me, Johnny.
Johnny (*wobbling*) Help me, Mum.

The crowd gasps and then is silent

Mum leaps forward to grab Johnny, dropping her letter

Mum (*as she leaps*) Johnny! No!

The crowd reacts

Mum pulls Johnny from the parapet, then sits on it

The sounds of the crowd subside to a hum

You great fool, frightening me like that. I feel sick. (*She looks over
the edge, screams and leaps up, putting her back against the wall
DS of the L window and covering her face*) I'm going to faint,
Johnny.
Johnny (*going to the L window and calling*) Here, pass me that chair
out.

Tyrone passes a small chair out to Johnny. Johnny puts the chair with its back to the wall DC

Johnny There. Sit on that.

Mum sits on the chair. Johnny sits on the parapet UL. *He picks up his letter and puts in on the parapet*

Tyrone exits during the following

Johnny Right. Here we are then.

Mum You don't mean to kill yourself do you? You're a good boy, Johnny. You've always been a good boy.

Johnny Oh? This is a different story from the one I usually hear, isn't it?

Mum I've tried to be a good mother to you, you know I have. But you exasperate me with all your big ideas and nothing behind them.

Johnny My ambitions, you mean.

Mum Ambitions? Daydreams more like. You drift about daydreaming and getting under my feet until I lose my temper.

Johnny I only need a bit of encouragement, but all you want is to get me out of the house.

Mum You're a grown man. A grown man shouldn't expect his mother to look after him. I've got my own life to lead.

Johnny Well you can get on and lead it now. I'm not stopping you any longer.

Mum What are people going to say about me if you jump off after all you've said?

Johnny I haven't said anything.

Mum You have. You've told that reporter down there that I'm no good.

Johnny No, I haven't. She asked me if you and me fight and I said yes. She asked if you always make me a hot dinner and I said no. She asked if the house is clean and tidy and I said no. She asked ——

Mum You don't need to go on. She's a slimy piece of work and it'll be in all the papers.

Johnny She's only from the local rag.

Mum What's Reg going to say?

Johnny I don't care what Reg says.

Mum You see? You're being selfish again. Well I care, and he's going to blame me. He's going to read what you've said in the papers and he's going to say it's my fault for the way I've brought you up.

Johnny It is your fault.

Mum I've slaved and struggled to make a home for you, and this is the thanks I get.

Johnny There's nothing to say thank you for.

Mum You're an ungrateful lout. You take after your father. All talk and no action. He should have taken you with him.

Johnny Whose fault was it that he didn't?

Mum Well, I know better now.

Johnny Now Reg wants to be rid of me.

Mum Reg doesn't want to share his home with a great idle layabout.

Johnny It's not his home, it's mine.

Mum All you do is hang around all day getting under his feet.

Johnny He's hanging around all day getting under mine.

Mum You're not the only one who's unemployed.

Johnny Don't I know it? Why else would Reg hang around you? You're his meal ticket.

Mum That's not true. You're jealous of Reg and me.

Johnny Yes, I am. You're supposed to be my mum, but you're too busy being his ——

Mum (*interrupting*) Don't you dare say that word again about your own mother. Don't you dare! It's a good job you ran out after saying that last night. Reg would have killed you.

Johnny Pity he didn't. Ugly great thug. I don't know how you stand him.

Mum Reg is very fond of me and I'm fond of Reg. I don't know what I'd do without him.

Johnny Reg! Reg! Reg! I'm sick to death of the sound of his bloody name.

Mum And don't you swear at your mother either, you horrible delinquent.

Johnny (*wildly*) I'll do more than bloody swear if I have my way. I'll take you with me.

Johnny moves forward, grabs his mother and pulls her towards the parapet edge, L. He climbs on to the parapet, still holding her arm

Mum Johnny! No! No!

Mum pulls free and staggers back so that she goes beyond the corner and finishes up on the narrow ledge below the R window. She screams and presses herself against the wall

During the following, Tyrone and PC Green enter the office and head for the R window

(*Terrified*) Johnny! Johnny! Oh, God help me.
Johnny (*from the parapet*) You cow! You old cow!

Tyrone and PC Green appear at the R window and lean out

PC Green You're all right, missis. Just stand still and recover yourself.
Mum I'm going to fall.
PC Green No you're not. Look straight ahead and edge this way slowly.
Mum I can't move.
PC Green Yes you can. It's only a couple of feet.
Mum No I can't. I'm falling. (*She screams*)
PC Green (*to Tyrone*) You be ready to grab her. (*He climbs out of the L window. He moves DS, his back to the audience. Passing Johnny*) I should give you a push, like you suggested. (*He moves on to the narrow ledge until he is alongside Mum, and can stretch his left arm across her*) Steady. I've got you. Move slowly to your right. Slowly. Slowly. No, don't look down.

They move along the ledge, Mum whimpering and shivering, until Tyrone can grab Mum's arm. He grabs her and she screams. Tyrone and PC Green bundle Mum over the sill and back into the room

That's cured my vertigo. (*He climbs through the window into the office*)

Mum leans out of the window. She is beside herself with rage and the after-effects of terror

Mum You nearly killed me, you little bastard. Wait 'til Reg hears about this. Don't expect him to let you over the doorstep when you try coming home, because as far as I'm concerned that's it, do you hear? I'm finished with you for good and all. You're a lazy, good-for-nothing, inconsiderate, cruel, selfish little pig. Go and find your father. Go and make a nuisance of yourself to somebody else. Just leave me alone to get on with my life in peace, because I never want to clap eyes on you again. Never.

Mum leaves the window. She remains in the office talking agitatedly to Tyrone and PC Green during the following

Johnny (*calling after her*) And I love you too, Mum! How about "Good Riddance" on my tombstone? (*He turns away and notices his letter. He picks it up*) Hey, Mum! You've forgotten your letter. (*He picks up the letter, goes to the R window and pokes his head in*) Mum! Your letter!

Mum ignores Johnny

Johnny puts the letter down inside the window and, forgetting that his is on the narrow ledge, turns away DS. His right leg swings out into space and he begins to fall. He shouts, then grabs for the windowsill with his left hand as his left leg buckles under him so that he is left dangling half on and half off the ledge

There are excited crowd noises from below; these continue appropriately until Johnny is rescued

Johnny Help! Somebody help me! I'm going to fall.

Tyrone and Mum come to the R *window and PC Green to the* L
window, where he starts to climb out

Tyrone Hang on, lad.

Tyrone grabs Johnny's arm. Mum leans out of the window

Mum You see? You can't even kill yourself properly. (*To Tyrone*)
Let him get on with it, because he's not coming back under my
roof.
Tyrone Shut up a minute. You're enough to drive anybody over the
edge.
Mum Oh! You wait 'til my Reg hears about you.

Mum crosses the office and exits

Johnny (*slipping further off the ledge*) Oh — oh — oh! I don't want
to die.
Tyrone (*struggling to hold on to Johnny*) Of course you don't, lad.
Remember when you're at rock bottom the only way to go is up.
Johnny Not from where I'm dangling, it isn't.
PC Green (*making his way along the narrow ledge*) I'm coming.
I'm coming. Oh, I wish I'd been a milkman like my father.

*PC Green reaches Johnny and helps him back on to the ledge during
the following*

The crowd below can be heard encouraging him

Got you. Up you come. Take it steady now or you'll have me over.

Johnny is now safely on the ledge

Now hang on to my shoulder and follow me.

They gradually edge L *until both are back on the wide ledge*

PC Green You're safe now, boy. Sit down a minute.

The crowd's noises subside to a hum of disappointment

Johnny (*sitting*) You saved my life. I guess that makes you a hero.
PC Green Does it? (*He grows visibly at the realization*) I suppose
it does. Never thought I'd dare. Heights terrify me.
Johnny (*in disbelief*) You're not frightened of heights!
PC Green Do you know, I don't think I am any longer. (*He climbs
on the parapet and poses on one leg*)

The crowd reacts

Look at me. After this lot I wouldn't mind trying a career as a stunt
man.
Johnny Now there's a life. I've dreamed of being in films. Are you
serious?
PC Green Dead serious. I'm not cut out to be a policeman.
Johnny I could have told you that. But are you sure you're cut out
to be a stunt-man?
PC Green After what I've just been through? Dead sure. You know
what? I've got a lot to thank you for. You've changed my life.
Johnny You'll get over it. You'll feel different when you've had
a cup of tea.
PC Green No. I'm going straight back to the Station now to hand
in my resignation.
Johnny And then?
PC Green Hollywood's where all the best stunt men go.
Johnny Hollywood! Would you consider taking a partner with
you?
PC Green You, you mean?
Johnny Yes, me. You owe it me.
PC Green All right. Why not?
Johnny Shake, partner.

They shake hands vigorously

Hollywood here we come! Wicked! I'll show my mum I'm not just a day-dreamer.

PC Green Now I'd better go and make my report.

Johnny Do you have to?

PC Green Regulations.

Johnny Pity. I thought we might discuss our future over a coffee in McDonald's

PC Green On second thoughts ——

PC Green claps Johnny on the back, indicating agreement

Johnny climbs into the office through the L window. PC Green moves to follow, then stops, turns, and tosses his black notebook over the parapet

Regulations. Who needs them?

PC Green follows Johnny out through the window

The crowd noises fade

Black-out

CURTAIN

FURNITURE AND PROPERTY LIST

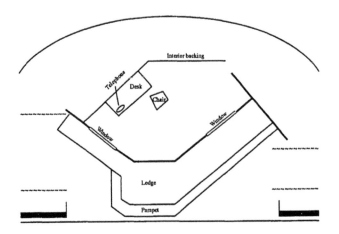

On stage:	Desk. *On it*: telephone
	One or two chairs
	Pad of paper and pen for **Johnny**
Off stage:	Window-cleaning cloth (**Tyrone**)
	Camera (**Judy**)
	Brown paper bag of grapes (**Eileen**)
Personal:	**Johnny**: envelope in pocket
	PC Green: black notebook

LIGHTING PLOT

Practical fittings required: nil
Exterior setting with interior backing. The same throughout

To open: General exterior and interior lighting

No cues

EFFECTS PLOT

Cue 11   **Johnny** climbs on to the parapet   (Page 23)
           Gasps from crowd

Cue 12   **Johnny** climbs down from the parapet   (Page 25)
           Disappointed noises from crowd

Cue 13   **Johnny** climbs on to the parapet   (Page 26)
           Crowd reaction

Cue 14   **Johnny** raises his leg   (Page 26)
           Crowd gasps

Cue 15   **Johnny**: "Help me, Mum."   (Page 26)
           Crowd gasps; then silence

Cue 16   **Mum**: "Johnny! No!"   (Page 26)
           Crowd reacts

Cue 17   **Mum** sits on the parapet   (Page 26)
           Crowd sounds subside to a hum

Cue 18   **Johnny** dangles off the ledge   (Page 30)
           Excited crowd noises

Cue 19   **PC Green** helps **Johnny** on to the ledge   (Page 31)
           Encouraging crowd noises

Cue 20   **PC Green**: "Sit down a minute."   (Page 32)
           Crowd noises subside to hum of disappointment

Cue 21   **PC Green** poses on one leg   (Page 32)
           Crowd reacts

Cue 22   **PC Green** follows **Johnny** through the window   (Page 33)
           Crowd noises fade